Author's Note

When I was younger, and to this day I've always wanted to be a singer, and songwriter. If you ask my best friend she'll say I'm wrong, but I'm not a very good singer and I can't play any instrument. (< that part is true). So I decided to call them 'poems'. Some are actual poems, some are songs, and I definitely think you can tell the difference between which ones were which. But all of these words of elegance could be songs.

I definitely want to thank Taylor Swift because I refer to some of her songs like *Death By A Thousand Cuts* and *Call It What You Want*, and even her song *Ivy* inspired one, but so did my heartbreak. I for sure don't deserve all of the credit, because I refer to some of Taylor Swift's masterpieces.

Some of these elegant words formed from my heartbreaks and I wrote them in my books, that will be out soon. I'll write down which book they're from so if it captures your attention you can be as excited as me for them to come out. These poems and elegant words will be in the order of which boy they were about, by the months, not the dates they were written. Which I think is really cool because you can see how I feel and think about a certain boy over time. The only thing that'll be a 'concern' is that sometimes when I'm heartbroken I just go straight to writing a book and no poems, and sometimes I just write elegant words, poems or songs. I even added some quotes I came up with for 'no reason'.

You'll even see some 'small' references to the books, however I won't tell you them, it'll be obvious anyways. Just know the books were written or being written before 'Elegant' was even born to be.

''Because I'm a mastermind.'' —Mastermind, Taylor Swift.

For, Taylor Swift,
Ms. Amazing Taylor Swift, you'll see this dedication
more than once.
I love you and thank you for being you and creating
all of your beautiful songs

And for my best friend, Leah Bean
Because I haven't dedicated anything to you... that
you know of, and who knows when that'll come out.
You're also my twin flame. We are a part of the
same soul

''No one wanted to play with me as a little kid so
I've been scheming like a criminal ever since.
To make them love me and make it seem effortless.
This is the first time I've felt the need to confess,
and I swear I'm only cryptic and Machiavellian
because I care.''
—Mastermind, Taylor Swift

August

(2022)

G.L.H

Contradicting Goodbye
G.L.H

Heartbreak. That's what we
Grew up with. But one still wants
Love, one just wants sex.
She(I) can't handle it, but she(I)
Likes him(you). So she(I) lights the
Candle at night. While he's(you're) on
Her(my) bed, holding her(me) tight.
And that's a contradicting goodbye.

2022
Date unknown
Somewhere around August 22nd–23rd
[EDIT: January 4th, 2024, Thursday.
11:38 P.M.]

He Said
G.L.H

He said that we'd
Be forever, just to say
We shouldn't be together.

I forgot that he loved
All the she's and all
Of the other girls, while
Being in love with me.

He sees us as
One happy couple. Two
Lovers, just to do a
Double take. And put the
Wooden stake to my
Heart. Breaking it all apart.

2022
Date unknown
Somewhere around August 22nd–26th
OR
Sometime past September

Attached
G.L.H

I guess your fake trust
Was only for real lust.
I really thought I could
Believe you. My friends
Did too. I had no clue
I'd get so attached to you.

You're one of few. But I'm
One too many for you. So you
Drop me for her. You can't see
the hurt on my face. Because I
Can't leave a trace of my past for
You to be proud of.

I thought we'd see the white dove
But of course you weren't sent
From up above. You were sent from
Hell. (Tell me) Did the devil approve of this?

This is a hard pill.
But so easy to swallow.
You'll follow her, I'll
Wallow in my tears.

2022 [EDIT: December 30th, 2023]

December

(2022)

T.C.B

Dress
T.C.B

Bought a dress for
A date. We never saw
Each other again.

I guess I'm a zero out of ten rate.
An unfaithful fate.
Because he loves her.

Should've seen this a
Mile ahead. Now my
Heart's broken, in a dress
I bought only
Meant to be taken off.

P.S. Thank you to Taylor Swift.
For the song *'Dress'*, because it
made me buy a dress, however no one
took it off me, except well for me haha.

2023
Date unknown
Has to be after January though
(my relationship w/ Dec. was falling apart around
this time)

I'm Sorry That I Miss You
T.C.B

Holidays are such a pain
When you're not a text away.
And I know I wasn't always the best to you,
But you weren't the best to me either.

You may ask me ''how?'' as your pride and
Ego wither away.
Because you always held it to a high standard
On a pedestal.
Now I'll tell you why to your how
As long as you take it as a true vow.

I never took your feelings into consideration
When I made fun of your height. And despite
What you may think I really did care about you
More than I ever acted.
I was always in defense.
You changed your pictures,
My friends found you on the internet. Don't think
they
Didn't tell me. This would lead to our end.
You always made me feel stupid, like I could never
Amount to anything. Could never be on your level.

So I destroyed what could've been

So you didn't get the chance to break what
would've been
So I destroy what should've been.

You'll tell your story, I'll tell mine,
Thinking we're both right.
The pride we held so bright
It blinded us without a fight or second thought.

Time taught me that we were both wrong.
Both at fault. Karma has me dealing with more
Arrogant pre-med kids, and karma has
You dealing with more deja-vu and heartbreak.
You're getting annoyed, I can tell.

Am I on your mind?
I find my way back to you. I hold back
As much as I could.
My friend told me to not text you,
You're an ex and so am I.

I'm sorry that I miss you,
I promise I'm trying not to.
We both deserve an apology,
We were both wrong at the time.

Months have passed since we last talked.
It's been a year since last December
And I still remember you,

And your poems, and how we loved to write them.
You're my secret home…land.

I'm sorry that I miss you,
I promise I'm trying not to.
I wish I could hear you say you miss me.
I don't think it'll come true
But I want it to.

Let's go back to December.
Back to what I remember
With you.

I'm sorry that I miss you,
I promise I'm trying not to.

I'm sorry I miss you,
I promise I'm trying not to.

November 23, 2023, Thursday
6:40 P.M. — 7:50 P.M.

April—June

(2023)

M.F.

Until You Had Me

M.F.

Loved me, until you
Really had me. Trapped
Under your heavy heart.
The wrong parts of me free
From your trap. Just like you wanted.
And now all of me is haunted.

And in seven months
It'll be ten months since you
Left me. And I'll be ten months
Clean. All you were was mean. But
I loved you, and all you had to do
Was stay. But I was 'in the way' of
Your 'happiness.'

I get that your past was coming back
To haunt you. And my life was coming
Back to save me. But I would've loved you
With everything I had to give. Despite
Your past and flaws that I never saw.
But you put the shiv in my heart either way.
Left me and left everything we could've became.

But how am I the one to
Blame?

I'll turn my phone off and
Try to live my life, instead I'll
Be a dead, weightless body.
I'll power my phone on, and
Try to find a new hobby, but instead
Cry, 'cause my texts are still empty.
But I remember when your name would
Show a beautiful blue heart.

I'll lie and say I don't love you
Anymore. But I'll cry about
You. Because to lose a love
I thought was pure, is
Impossible.

The reality was you loved me
Until you really had me. You loved me, but
When you really had me, you left.
Now you're a living ghost. The
Cruel host in my broken, fallen, heart.

And in seven months it'll
Be ten months until you left me.
And I'll be ten months clean.
You became a ghost, but I have to
Pay the price? For a difference I didn't
Ask for.

I'm screaming in the rain:

''Oh where the hell did you go
Mateo?'' The pain fills my lungs.
My head once held high, sinking
So below, hung heavy like my heart.

I'll sob and my voice'll become raw.
''Oh where the hell did you go, Mateo?''
While I still fear I'll see you at the coffee
Shop. You took your poisoned silver
Spear to my bright, beating heart.
But I'll still be screaming:
''Oh where the hell did you go, Mateo?''
Because I loved you so.

October 11th, 2023, Wednesday
4:15 P.M.

Alki Beach
M.F.

I'm all dressed up, only
To go nowhere. What did I do?
What did I do? To deserve this?
I never was his, was I?
I was always his, he was never mine.

His touch all over me, butterflies
Are still alive. All of his knives are
Still stuck in my back. It's okay. It's
Only death by a thousand cuts. Something
I've healed from. From every boy I've loved.

I'd look up above, and see the pastel skies
With bright stars faded in. Matching moon
Phases and constellations. Made for us,
Connected to look like us. They call it love. If
Only you agreed.

You can call it what you want.
But I saw the love in his eyes. I saw
The look of love in his smirk. I didn't
Know I'd miss it when it was out
Of my reach.

No more beach walks
No more red flannel hugs

When I'm cold.
No more moments of being
Bold.
No more of his hold, unless
It's on my heart.
Because he took every part of
Me away with his unsaid goodbye.

And heartbreak makes time fly
When you're counting the months
Of how long you've been gone.
Because there's no more fun
To look forward to.

And I'm in love with a coward
Who can't say goodbye to the girl he
Loved, a week before her birthday.
A few days before she leaves for
Vacation.

Stayed in the middle of the lake
Waiting for the wake of the
Dying love of my heart to be
Over. Get the resurrection of my
Familiar heartbreak. I'm not a slut.
I'm just a girl who believed her
Boyfriend's affection that was
Called love.

I'd look up above, and see the pastel skies
With bright stars faded in. Matching moon
Phases and constellations. Made for us,
Connected to look like us. They call it love. If
Only you agreed.

All dressed up with nowhere to go. Hair bow
All tied up in my curled hair, to match
My curved body you loved so much.
A love beats so big in my chest, it
Matches my big eyes that got you so
Mesmerised, that you loved so much.
Heart so damagingly pierced from your
Unsaid goodbye to match my nose and ears.
The features you loved so much.

Head concussed from your love
Going head first into it. Just
Like how you first met me.

I'll never walk Alki Beach again,
But he's probably taken a
Million girls there, for,
Just because.

His touch all over me,
Butterflies still alive.
All of his knives are still
Stuck in my back. It's okay.

It's only death by a thousand cuts.
Something I've healed from. Let's
Go again. From all the boys I've loved.

I'd look up above, and see the
Pastel skies with bright stars
Faded in. Completed moon
Phases and constellations
Made for us. Connected to look
Like us. Everyone called it love.
If only you agreed.

October 27th, 2023, Friday
1:11 A.M. — 1:25 P.M.

Fool's Gold
M.F.

I look at our old texts
Now that you're my ex.
One of them. I begged you
To stay in a harsh way.
You probably partied that day,
Got drunk like you always do.
Leaving me with my say.

I know I'm falling for your
Fool's gold. But the chokehold it
Has on me. I'll keep falling. All
The ocean waves calling, calming the
Love that crashes ashore. Pulling us
Back to reality.

You moved me away from the
Door when we slept. Took you a bit,
But you did it, even if it confused you.
Now I want to know who's taken all
My nighttime spots. No one's taken yours.
It's still cold, except my heartbreak's
Leaked, only keeping it barely warm.

How many girls swarm your studio
Apartment? In your air bed. With your
Twenty–five year old girl roommate?

Tell me baby, is it her?

You're only twenty–three, you
Loved me when I was eighteen, almost
Nineteen, but you'd never know, 'cause
You left me nine days before my birthday
Because you were never mine, but I was
Always yours.

Crying, screaming, on all fours
Dancing, crying, smiling on all
The floors. I stare up at the
Ceiling not really believing
That you're gone.

So long! I know I visit your head
All the time! I'll put us in the limelight
Without a second thought,
with a millionth fight.

What do you tell your friends?
Did you tell them how we *really*
Came to an end? Waiting at my door,
Like the poor poor soul I am.
Your heart really is a cruel cold.

I know I really fell for your fool's
Gold. But I love the chokehold it has
On me, and I'll keep falling. Ignoring

All the Taylor Swift callings, on the radio.
Telling me to run away! I'll miss the screaming,
And kissing in the rain. About how I'll be lying
On the cold, hard ground, of how I should've
Known he was trouble when he walked
Into my life.

But I strife for that fool's gold.
That's what got me sold. It brought
Me back to life. It bought off my
Grief of old me.

Tell me baby! Who sleeps in all my spots,
On your air bed!? Does she have a better
Head? (On her shoulders).

(Fuck!) You're only twenty-three
And you had all of me. Baby can't you see?
It was all meant to be.
(Maybe? Not really?)
I know it's silly. But I also love that I turned
Into a what–if fantasy in your brain.

Pull me from your memory
And kiss me in the rain again.
Love me until we're warm.

How many girls swarm your
Studio apartment? In your air

Bed? With your twenty–five year
Old girl roommate? Tell me baby,
Is it her?

Does the new girl have a better head?
(On her shoulders)

I know I fell for your fool's gold.
But god I love the chokehold
It has on me. And I'll keep falling,
Stupidly ignoring all the Taylor Swift
Callings, on the radio. Telling me I'll
Miss the screaming and kissing in
The rain.
(Please take this pain away)
About how I'll be lying on the cold
Hard ground, about how I should've
Known you were trouble when
You walked in my life.
(Please take this pain away)

Crying and screaming on all fours!
Dancing, crying, smiling, on all
The floors! I stare up at the ceiling,
Not really believing that you're gone.

You're only twenty-three, and you
Had all of me.
Baby can't you see?

I know it's silly.
But I also love that I
Turned into a what-if, a fantasy
Just for you babe.

October 27th, 2023 — October 28th, 2023
Friday and Saturday
10:30 something P.M. — 12:29 A.M.

Lovebird
M.F.

All, all of the first words
You said to me repeat in
My head. You're a dead dead
Love.

(Sing me a song, and I'll fall in love)

If I sing you a love song,
Will you fall in love with me?
Take me to Pike Place and
Alki Beach? Kiss my face in
The pouring rain. And hold me
On the brick street. Never to be more
Than three feet away from me?

Please picture you and me, us
In the way, the way we're supposed
To be. Wrapped in my old bed,
With my cat on our chest.
Our messed up hair heads.
And never go away.
Don't play with my heart instead.
Just love me for who I am, as I
Do with you.

And when the next guy asks me

To sing for him, I'm reminded of
How you're my ex, never to be
The same. And watch as my
Heartbreak ricochets off
My chest, hurting me more.

(Sing me a song, and I'll fall in love)

If I sing you a love song
Will you fall in love with me?
Take me to Pike Place and
Alki Beach? Kiss my face in
The pouring rain. And hold me
On the brick street. Never to be more
Than three feet away from me?

I'll be your perfect songbird,
You're the only one that's made
My beautiful melody feel heard.
Seal your promise with a love stare
And a love kiss.

We'll switch, I'll become the
Weeping willow tree. You'll be
The song bird, leave me for her.
The third party.
I'll be stuck, roots bed down,
I'll wait for you, slowly dying.
Repeating your beautiful,

Lying melody.

Did all the things you wanted to see.
Became the girl you wanted me to be.
Who I'm supposed to be. All by my
Design, yes, even before your resign.
I still hold on like a child with
Their blanket.

One day I'll say ''Fuck it'' and let
You go without knowing, and that'll
Be the sweet release. You'll get
Your bad luck streak.
I won't be yours and so won't she.
But for now I still am. Maybe she
Is or isn't.

(Sing me a song, and I'll fall in love.)

So I'll still sing you my
Heart's love melody.
And maybe you'll still
Be in love with me.
But please don't take me
To Alki beach.
But maybe still kiss me at
Pike Place Market.
And please still kiss me
In the pouring rain.

And hold me on brick street.
Never to be more than
A heartbeat away.

November 4th, 2023, Saturday
10:40 P.M.

Every Part Of Me (Elegant)
M.F.

You break my heart
Like every boy from before.
It still hurts past the core of
My heart. It's in every part of me.

I'm fucked for life, I know it.
While you're all tucked in with her.
Listening to her purr in happiness
It's torture, I swear. So happy to see you
Bear the thought of not caring.

You broke my heart like I've never
Known. The pain in my chest is insane
I know for you it's cold, you're so vain
That you're just glad you're being mentioned.
With no intention to think how
Sad you made me.

Tell me my 'sweet' baby which
Pretty lady paid or persuade you to
Kill my heart? Who made you forget
Every part of me? Was it
Addictive Opie? I know she made you
Feel like 'goodfella'. Like you hit jackpot.

I guess losing everyone you loved
Taught you nothing. Because
Opie's *high* love never went away.

I know it's very low of me to call
Out your *addiction* for your ex 'love'
But it was low of you to blow me off
Nine days before my nineteenth birthday.
Called me beautiful just to never show
Up to our date.
''Must've been fate,'' I used to say to my friends
when I met you. I thought you felt it too.

Still stuck in the heartbreak.
I'm counting the months of how long
I've been standing at the wake. Sometimes
I get the courage to take a step away
But I don't like my feet being cold
So I'm back to being
Next to the beautiful casket
Of us.

I've been at the wake for five months
And counting. Oh baby, why'd you have to leave?
Lead me on a dead–end trail. Pull
The veil over my head but you're not there.
I look around but it's like you've disappeared
Into thin air. Like you didn't even care.

I've been at the wake for five months
And counting. I'm no longer
Fallen in love, you knew
Every part of me. You tear my heart
Into a million pieces and you didn't
Even care.

I'm no longer
Fallen in love, you knew
Every part of me. It's like I'm
Metaphorically naked,
Still can't believe you
Faked it.

November 25, 2023, Saturday
(sometime between 1:46 P.M. — 2:56 P.M.)

Trepidation
M.F.

I was in a state of trepidation when
I fell in love with you.
Thinking you'd leave me in desolation.

I cried loudly over the shower.
Isolation is what you put me through,
Put my heart on the newly cleaned shelf.

People say it's for the better
But if it was I don't think I would've
Written that three–paged poetic letter.
That I sent to your apartment's
Address that I vividly remember.

Where I cooked for you
Where you had me hooked.
You were my life–line
I made your happiness shine.
I thought you were mine
Did I miss the sign?

I need to hear you say I'll be fine
Just one more time.

I had trepidation at
Pike Place Market on

May 8th. Didn't know it'd come
True and I'd be in a state of
Desolation.

I'm doing a celebration of what should've
been our six month anniversary in
Isolation.

The precipitation coming down
On us, while I had trepidation
About us. Love and lust must be
The potion for your reasoning
For leaving me in isolation.

I want to go home.
With us in bed, comb
Your fingers through my
Out–grown bangs.
Please take me home,
Please take me home.
I miss my home.

Take away my desolation,
I'm sorry I felt trepidation.

I want to go home with
us in bed, comb your fingers
Through my out–grown bangs.
Please take me home,

Please take me home
I miss my home.

November 26th, 2023, Sunday
10:06 P.M. — 10:26 P.M.

Surreal Mythicality
M.F.

The coalescence of our soul
And bodies when we kissed
In the rain. Your red flannel keeps
Me warm and heartbroken underneath
The same grey sky.

Before we even knew this would
Be our last goodbye. The pain
In my heart lights up again. I can't
Help but do polite screams and cries.
You follow me into my
Junoesque dreams.

So surreal. The heartbreak
You put me through is a
Grotesque mess. You make
It hard to forget you. I wish I
Could haunt you too. Taunt all
The girls you'll cruelly trap with
All your lies. I hope they see me in
Their pretty pretty eyes, and leave
You with a million goodbyes too.

Your voracious kisses as we
Held our loving faces.

All the places you promised to take us
Have hidden traces of you, that I always
Seem to find.

I thought the invisible string would
Bind us for life. But instead
We're trying to untie us, as we're still
Closely intertwined.
Even if we're not in eye–sight.

You promised that you
Wouldn't bite. I saw your eyes
Get wide when I made a life decision
After I met you.

I know you felt guilty too.
Is that why you're extra blue?
And to leave me without a word?
No message on a bird.

You'll watch your life slowly
Become something you hate.
As you picture what our
relationship would've been.

A surreal mythicality it is.
You'll miss the coalescence of our
Personalities.

You'll follow me into my
Junoesque dreams.
My heart ripped at its stitched
Seams. A grotesque sight to
See and feel.

A surreal mythicality
I'll admit.

I'll follow you into your
Grotesque dreams, being the only
Junoesque thing you'll ever see.

December 3rd, 2023, Sunday
12:51 A.M. — 1:33 A.M.

Getaway Car
M.F.

Stay up until the
Sunrise, left the birthday
Surprise at home.

The strong air freshener
Scent in your banged
Up gold car. You didn't
Live close nor very far.
''Poor girl,'' your roommate
And friends say, as they laugh
At what you did to me.

The morning of the continuation of
Our dates, the strong air freshener
Scent. All stained into my brain.
With my sense of belonging with you.

The sound of rain scares me now.
I thought we were the perfect
Pair. But you didn't want to share
Me with your time and liquor.
The empty cans and bottles
Everywhere.

''I'm twenty–three and she's
twenty–five. Of course we're going

to drink." Is what you said to me.
In the living room of your studio.

I loved you though.
So I stayed concerned and
Scared for the both of us.
As I think about our summer.

You didn't live close nor
Very far, if you ask me so.

I reminisce you
Holding me as I cried.
Wanting to leave this place.
You said we can go in a little bit.
Just you and I. I miss you.
Didn't know you'd wreak
Havoc on us.

And I never got to admit
That I love you. I know you
Probably wouldn't have
Said it back. 'Cause you lack
Truth to your words and promises.

Remember the getaway car?
How you promised
We'd go far, so very far.

Leave this place and
Go to the very small
Old town. Down to the other
Side of the evergreen state.

Never saw our doomed
Fate. Leaving my unfinished
Heart on the dinner plate.

I shake as I cry out of the
Hot showers. Stare mindlessly
At the pretty flowers by
The cold lake. Missing your
Beautiful warm hold.

I wish you told me your
Intentions. Instead your only
Mentions were that
I was your Life–line.
I made your happiness shine.
Like you've never seen before.

It's almost like you said
You loved me. So you
Shoved me out the door.
Never to see those pastel
Pinks ever again.

So I just sink to

The ground. My heart
Never to be found the same.

The strong air freshener scent,
The feeling that I belonged.
In your banged up gold car.
You didn't live close nor very
Far. ''Poor girl,'' your
Roommate and friends say,
as they laugh at what you
Did to me.

This was our ends to meet.
But the invisible string is taking
A seat before it makes us meet
Again.

Giving you a second chance
You'll never forget.

Remember the getaway
Car? How you promised
We'd go far, so very far.

Leave this place, go to
The small old town. Just
Down to the other side of
The evergreen state.

But instead you tore
Apart my beautiful heart.
Leaving it unfinished
On the porcelain plate.
Leaving an unremarkable scar.

December 4th– December 5th, 2023
Monday–Tuesday
(11:28 P.M. — 4:57 P.M.)
(EDIT: 5:00 P.M.)

Noah Kahan
M.F.

I know I say this a lot.
But baby it's the toll I pay
For my heartbreak. It's the
Transaction fee from your
Withdrawal.

How I listened to
Noah Kahan the day we
Kissed in the rain. Without
Knowing the stupid
Pain of that unsaid goodbye.

Inside my house, away
From the pouring rain
And away from you. Putting
On my new lip tint. As you
Look back at the stint of our
Relationship, in the getaway car.

Now all I have is the memory
Of June 10th, the coffee house,
And Noah Kahan and his folk songs.

You choke on the love I gave you.
And maybe that's why you left.
Nine days before my birthday. After

Saying that you loved me, that I was
Gorgeous and beautiful everyday you
Could. Up until June 23rd. I know I
Say it a lot but what else can I
Do, babe?

I gave you my all,
I loved you past your
Grotesque past and flaws.
Something I'm sure people
Ditched you for. But that
Didn't mean you had to
Pitch your softball to my
Heart. So it can go to my
Medical chart. For when the
Doctor asks about my failing heart.

I'm not as lucky as you.
I can't go sailing past
Vashon and Mercer Island
To go up to Bremerton. Where you
Partied that day. Where you left me
With my trebmlin' say. Bet you never
Complained about all the driving you
did that day. Like how you did with me
On all of our dates.

I pay the transaction fee
Of your withdrawal.

Of how I had to crawl across
My bathroom floor because I
Was too weak to move. From the
Heartbreak you put me through.

And I wonder if your boys
And roommate will cheer you on
As you drink your millionth beer.
When you'll read this, they'll
Say: ''Wow, good for you.
Do you see how you had her
Hooked for you. How you made
Her still talk about it to this day?''

And all I can say is:
All I have is the memory of you
On June 10th, the coffee house,
Noah Kahan and his folk songs.

You'll choke on the love
I gave you. You'll
Go back to your apartment
On Broadway street. And
Wonder how and what we
Could've became.

And I wonder if your
Boys and roommate will

Cheer you on, as you drink your
Millionth beer, or twisted tea.
They'll cheer you on
About how you broke my heart
But I was only eighteen.

December 9th, 2023, Saturday
1:02 P.M. — 1:32 P.M.
[EDIT: 3:20 P.M. & 3:25 P.M.]

Gorgeous
M.F.

You used to always call me
Gorgeous and beautiful.
But that was before I knew you
Were porous about us.

How on June 4th you said
You were sorry about your
Abrupt cancellation on our
Non–boring restaurant
Destination date. You'd tell
Me, I'm okay, because you know
How I hate to eat in front of people.

But instead I only got
''Sorry,'' and that your depression
Was what was repressing us.

I know you suppressed me
Farther than the back of
Your mind.

But *'I wish you'd say*
You were sorry one last time.
I didn't deserve this. And it
Sucks because you get to
Be okay, and when I think I'm

Okay, I'm not. And you break
My heart all over again'.

This is a text I never sent,
But it's all typed up. And maybe
If I ever get drunk I'll send it.
But I know it won't happen
Anytime soon.

I wish I could drunk call you.
Hear your voice in real time. And
Not the voicemail you sent on
May 20th. When worry struck my
Mind and soul. But replaced
With relief and happiness
When I knew you were okay.

You used to call me gorgeous
And beautiful. But that was before
I knew you were porous about us.
And now when others say I'm—
I can't believe it.

But if you were to call me
I'd answer immediately.
And I don't care if that means
I haven't learned my lesson.
Because you were the best thing
In my nineteen years of life.

And I don't care if that makes
Me overdramatic.

December 9th, 2023, Saturday
8:42 P.M.

I Didn't Deserve This.
M.F.

Met a boy in August(2023).
To try to move on from
You. He only made things
Worse. It's like I'm
Living some god damn curse
Of never being put first.

He did things that I can't
Bring myself to say. But when
I was left on his Queen sized bed
I stared at the grey wall. Silent
Tears fell.

And the only thing
I could think of was our first
Date. And I told you it
Happened once. And as I stared
At his grey wall, it happened
Twice.

How I just wanted to be
Wrapped in your arms.
Tell me I'm safe now.
Instead of an ice pack,
Redness, and heartbreak.

All I could think of
Was you. And how I
Want to be safe in your
Warm arms.

I didn't deserve this.
And I didn't deserve
What happened in
August. But it hurts
Like I did.

And when I'm alone
I breakdown. I cry so hard.
I look around my room.
Not knowing where to
Look, or who to look
For. Or who to call.

I haven't shown anyone
What my mind really has
Going in it. Only the
Elegance it creates. In
Riddles so only I understand.
And I'm scared if I do, they'll
Runaway like you.

My body is haunted by August.
I didn't deserve this. But it
Hurts like I did.

And all I wish is that
I'm back in your
Arms, safe again.

December 9th, 2023, Saturday
8:53 P.M — 9:06 P.M.
[EDIT: 10:15 P.M.]

Made Me
M.F.

You share the same birthday
As my brother. C'mon babe
You know this isn't fair.
To tear my heart. Make me
Write love songs about you.
Make me feel like this
Is the ideal love I deserve.

Make me believe we're golden.
Even when you're holdin' me.
Just to never see us through.

What even went through
You're head? Who the hell
Do you think you are?
''But babe you're just so far.''
Making me think I'm not
On par with you. Truth
Is you didn't want to
Love me like I do…
With beautiful you.

You'll get what you
Deserve. We all do.

I'll only grow. And become

Someone known. Your
True colours will be shown.
Everyone will know
The truth.

Just admit it.
I know what you're
Thinking. We can share
The same mind as you.
I just choose not to.

Flew out of state
To get away from you.
To hangout with my best
Friend. Before it's too
Late and I get lost in
The memory of you.

C'mon babe. You
Knew it was wrong
To tempt fate.
But you did it anyway.

December 19th, 2023, Tuesday
12:23 P.M. [At work] — 9:27 P.M.

Late Night Mornings
M.F.

I walk to work in the rain,
The constant pain follows
Me. Reminding me of when
You kissed me. Telling me
That you missed me, that
You wish you could still
Kiss me.

The traffic lights twinkle,
Not giving a single answer
Of I'll be okay. It's up to
Anyone's say. I wished
You stayed.

I walk to work in the rain,
The constant pain follows
Me. Of you putting the
Strain on us. You're not
Some saint, you never
Claimed to be. But can't you
See that we were fine. You
Didn't need to put a level
Nine heartbreak.

For whose sake?
What's the give?

What's the take?
My heart's at stake.

I walk to work in the rain
With hazed pain following
Me. I know you're not
Fazed by any of this.
It's been six months. But
The early morning, meaning
Our late nights. Traffic reminds
Me of you.

Tears of mystical blue
Trail down my face. How
We used to joke about me
Wearing the veil. How my
Name would match yours.
Instead fame will take me.
Someone else will catch my
Heart. But I remember when
You held it, after you taped the broken
Pieces together.

You'll love her. And I'll love him
But why couldn't it just be us?

I walk to work in the rain.
The same damn pain follows
Me. I'll go to all the holiday

Parties, and talk about you.
Say I'm not in love with you.
Talk about my projects
That you inspired. Get
Congratulated. But none
Of it matters, 'cause I'm
Not with the one I was fated
With.

December 15th, 2023, Friday
5:39–something– A.M.—5:57 A.M.
[At work] [EDIT: 11:30 A.M.]

The Louvre (French)
M.F.

I hate the chase.
You love my face.
You love to trail the kisses
Down my body. And I did
Too. You leave, giving you
A clean slate. Having my heart
Break, for you selfish sake.

You fell in love with me.
Just admit it. The way you
Fit into my hand, into me.

Was this your plan, all along?
To love me for this long, just
To be gone without telling me.

I thought you were my soulmate
But you told me you were a faux fate.
With the way you left.

Our perfect hands tied. And I
Want to blame my life after
You on you. But how can I?
When thou aren't even here.
Don't you just have a sheer of
Regret. I thought you were mine.

Or was that just a line?

I've run out of pages in my
Notebook, writing about you.
And the heartbreak you put me
Through.

People will go to the Louvre
And say I should be displayed
There. My heartbreak is
Already known. Might as well
Show the story of what you're
Prone to do.

That my heart is owned
By you. And I don't want it
To. You should be displayed.
Have your selfish ways never
Fade. Have people ask you
Questions, on why you did
What you did.

December 27th, 2023, Wednesday
6:29 A.M. — 9:07 A.M.
[At work]

You Were My Home
M.F.

I want to say
''Take me home.''
And you'd take me
Back to your place.
Instead of saying
''Which one?''

And if I knew our
Ending would be
The case. I would've
Never texted you.

And in everyone's
Point of view. I
Was lovestruck.
And I knew I was.
I thought I was
Your first pick.
Making me lovesick.
But it was worth it.

Your hand fit into mine.
If only you held it
All of the time.
And not just when other
Boys were around.

So they could never
Pick me. So I could
Never be fixed. So
I could never be found.

You were my home.
And I thought I was
Yours too, based off
Your words. I should've
Been more.

You tore my heart.
Made love taste
Sweet–tart.

I've said it once,
And twice. And I'll
Say it again and again.
Because of the
Convincing you did.

You were my life–line.
I made your happiness
Shine. Like you've never
Seen before. All the
Unfulfilled promises to
Take me to Pike Place.

You kissed my face
In the rain.

Called me beautiful
Up until June 23rd.
That's when I never
Heard from you again.

You never said an
Apology. And you
Fucked me up
Psychologically.

You were my home.
Loved me like I've
Never known before.
Ruined me like I've known
All too well. But hurt me
Like I've never known.

And you took me
Away from home.
You took away my
Home.
You were my home.

And you took me
Away from home.
You took away my

Home.
You were my home.

And you took me
Away from home.
You took away my
Home.
You were my home.

December 19th, 2023, Tuesday
10:13 P.M. — 10:29 P.M.

Quotes, Other poems, and
Extra elegant words.

Incandescent Glow
(Nothing too bad. Just a crush I got over)
(A little dramatic if you ask me.)

Did I once make your
Heart flutter? In the
Night, in the glow of
Late morning. On
All the days we saw
Each other.

All of it, is a confusing
Haze. I miss the times
Where I thought maybe
One day you would be mine.

I forgot to keep my heart
On the line. On proper
Track. Now I'm
Back to picking myself
Apart. Questioning
All the things she does
Better than me.

Tell me does she do
The same? I'll tell
You: I can't blame her,
For falling in love with
You. There's nothing to

Hate. That's never up to debate.

I just wish you could
Be mine. I wish we
Would have the right time.
Our hands tied tight.

I still remember my first
Thoughts when I first saw you.
There was a glow in me that
I thought I would never see
Again. But it was a deal
Never to be made. So with
The heavy my heart became,
The glow below my heart
Grew a sad shade.

I never told you about
That beautiful glowing
Light, because I didn't want
To lose the light in between
Us. It was so robust.
We were so incandescent
The other birds even saw
It. Chirping about it amongst
The breadcrumbs.

Now I'm all numb.

Does she do the same?
I know I said I hope
She does. I put my truth aside
For your happiness. For no
Immatureness. And I
I meant all the words
I said.

I just wished it worked
Out and that you're very
Happy with me.

But maybe that's not
How our story goes. I know
You said you don't want
To lead me on. But can't
You see that you did.
You acted as if it didn't
Happen. And if I never
Woke up to that text
I wouldn't've thought
Twice about your sweet hellos.

Because that incandescent glow
Is still there.

And if I'm being honest
I think it'll always be there.
That incandescent glow

Will just be hidden a little.
We'll be just friends.
That's how this story ends.

October 3rd, 2023 — October 4th, 2023
Tuesday — Wednesday
Time unknown.
[EDIT: December 21st, 2023, Thursday
9:29 P.M.]

Body
(Someone who is unimportAnt. But so there is no mix-up, we'll Just Call him August(2023))

I try to wash my
Delicate body of you.
The hot water and
Ice packs burn my
Skin.

At least I can say ''la fin''
With you. I begged you
To stay even after
Everything you did.

You'll leave a bad trace
And every time I turn to
Face behind me
I get the memory of
The wasted nights spent.

Date unknown.
[EDIT: December 21st, 2023, Thursday
9:45 P.M.]

From ''Fallen In Love''

Well you waited this long,
Welcome to the Fallen In Love
Elegance.

G.L.H
''Gold Rush Conman.''

There he was living in my memories.

I didn't want him there, giving me a haunted past.

My heart's dusty ol' cast just got taken off.

*Because he left it cold when he's the one that lit the
golden fire.*

*Warming me up in places I didn't think was
possible.*

Told them, everyone, I'm okay.

When I'm everything less than.

Because I thought he was a better man.

I try not to cry, try not to let the tears glow.

But they flow a shade of sad, down my face.

In the one place I thought I was safe.

Because he was never the better man.

He was nothing more than a gold rush conman.

Stealing my heart, leaving me in cold, bruised parts.

He's the boy I loved in August.

He pretended to give me a beautiful love just so he could get his peaceful lust.

But he was the boy I loved in August.

G.L.H
''Eighteen''

I was young.

Just eighteen.

His birthday was on the sixteenth.

He's in his twenty-teens.

Maybe I was another scheme.

But can I ask why just me?

Why just me, why just me?

From "Every Part Of Me"

(Author's Note)
So here's another fun fact, and interesting backstory
to the Every Part Of Me elegance.
I wrote Fallen In Love because I was heartbroken,
and finished the book right before I fell in love. I
started to write Every Part Of Me because I was in
love and continued to write it because I was
heartbroken.
Now there isn't much poetry, but there is beautiful
elegance. And more short stories I started writing. It
was more like I had a story to tell with M.F.
Because I started writing right after our first date.
So I will show all the short stories and drafts I came
up with when I was in love. Including the start of
Every Part Of Me.
So, with that being said, Enjoy!
And welcome to the
Every Part Of Me
Elegance!

Beautiful

Him.

Beautiful

She was more beautiful than the rising sun, and

the birds that sang along. She was more beautiful than all of the beautiful things she loved. She was beautiful even if she didn't see it. Even if she didn't believe it. The way her eyes lit up, the way she smiled when she talked about all her favourite things. Beautiful like summer waters, autumn colours, winter snows, and spring flowers.

She laid her beautiful head on my chest, where her beautiful hair laid, scattered. Her laptop holding a half blank page. Her beautiful written words only made me think she was even more beautiful. The words perfectly put together. Elegant, was something that her mind was. But if you ask me, her mind was elegantly beautiful.

I loved her beautifully.

''You know you're missing a key, right?'' I tell her.

''I know. I can't afford a new laptop though. The backspace is broken too. If I wasn't going through it. Recovering financially, and physically from my injury. I'd actually go get a new laptop. I know it hurt her. And her hurt, hurt me too.

''It's okay, ma belle. Everything will come together like puzzle pieces forming a beautiful picture.'' She sniffled, and I knew she wanted to cry.

''I just don't feel like myself anymore. I feel like I'm losing myself. Like my life is getting away from me, and it's never going to come back to save me.'' I place my hands on her jaw and lift her head up slightly so I can kiss her beautiful lips. ''Don't think like that. How about this, think of something, anything, and we'll go do it right now.'' She kisses me again before thinking.

''Can we watch the stars? I think they're so beautiful in the summer.'' I smile.

''Of course.'' We left my apartment and drove down to the nearest field I could possibly find. I laid the blanket on top of the flowery field. Augustine watched the stars and soon enough she fell asleep in my arms. She looked so beautiful, like her mind. I never want her to know how grotesque mine was. Because her beautiful mind would become corrupt, like mine.

Her

Corrupt

He was so handsome that my mind would stop working from his beauty. He would never know how corrupted my mind and life was. He was the source of colour to my grey world.

(May 12th, 2023)

———————

Author's note:

And that was it for that one.

I was in love and couldn't bring myself to ever touch it again.

Just One Month....

The one month rule. For every relationship,

every feeling of ''love'' I ever had, it lasted just one month. Nothing more, nothing less. With the first boy it hurt, the second it didn't. With this one, the third one, I was hurt. It hurt because this one made it seem like this time it was going to be different. Maybe I'm the problem. Because I'm nineteen dating ''men'' in their early twenties.

I knew that if this one didn't work I'd be done for. I didn't care how young I was, it felt horrible when ''men'' left, after they made you feel like you're their world. Even if it was just for one month. Maybe I should change everything about myself. Maybe I'd be more desirable, maybe I should be like all the other girls I get left for. Find out what makes them so amazing, and do what they do.

The first one found me, and liked me. The second one said I had a personality, the third one complimented me. All had one thing in common. They left for better girls. This is a simple champagne problem. There were worst things happening in other people's lives— hell my life. But

I didn't want to focus on them. I wanted to forget my problems. Maybe if I did things I never did on a norm I'd forget them or somebody would see me calling for help. (But no one ever did. No matter what I did).

Maybe I asked for too much when I wanted someone to love me. Maybe we all got lost in translation. I spoke heart, they spoke whore.

''Oh come on Juliette you can't be mad at me—''

''The hell I can!!'' I yell in the chill, autumn, New York night. ''If you made plans with me why would you ignore me for the whole day! Not pick up my phone calls!''

''We've only been going out for a month!''

''So what? That means I can't rely on you? That I can't believe you when you say something! You can't just say you want to go out with me then ignore my text and calls! That's lying you fucking prick!''

I blink the tears out of my eyes. I set the champagne on the kitchen counter. Chandler was twenty-three. He said that he saw things going further with me, that he really, *really* liked me. Saw something with me. Maybe he just said that so I'd have sex with him. And if he were to ever hear me say or think this he'd probably say: *That's not true, I really liked you.*

What a shame I'm fucked up in the head, because I believed him. It worked. Sometimes I hate myself and how weak I can be. I don't mean to be, I think I just got ahead of myself when I believed his words.

I don't want to hurt you, I'm starting to really like you.

I'm sure I won't remember him in a few months if this doesn't work out. Or I'll cry for ten months, just like with the first one. This whole situation is sad, really.

(I remembered and loved him for all of the months)

I thought that maybe one night I'd cook for us, and we'd have a romantic night that ended with us in each other's arms. But it's my fault. He said he had feelings for me, so I believed him. He complimented me on the streets of New York, so I believed him. My fault, truly.

How dare I believe someone, how dare I trust someone after what happened the last few times. I should know better. As my friends and my inner monologue,— my greatest enemy, tell me.

Sat on the New York bench, I sniffle. ''Fuck you—''

''Oh come on Juliette.''

''You're a liar!'' My voice breaks.

''Why? Because I didn't drive you back to my place for a date?''

''No!'' I get up off the bench, and so does Chandler.

''No!?''

''No! It's because you said we could go out and I even asked you what time you said after 12:00! I called you at 3:30, then at 4:45! Then again at 5:32!! You ignored my text and all my calls! So fuck you, you fucking liar!'' We're screaming at this point. ''And it's the fact that you did this to a different girl who you were meant to go on a date with, and then you said you wanted to see me instead! So how can I believe you, that you weren't doing anything!?''

''I have fucking depression, Juliette! What do you want me to do—''

''Oh fuck you! So do I, but I don't fucking ignore you or treat you horribly because of it! Face it Chandler you're not the only one in the world! Other people suffer from it!'' We argued more before I said something I deeply regret. Chandler struggled with drugs, he was sober now, but we both have issues. Mine were anger at this moment.

"Juliette stop being so dramatic!"

"Oh shut the fuck up, Chandler! You're a fucking liar. Get the fuck away from me, go back to doing drugs and blame all your problems on that!" I said before I walked away. Tears slipped out, because how could I say something like that?

I broke the champagne glass, cutting my hand. The half empty flute spilt on the hardwood kitchen floor "Shit." I say to myself, as I bend down to pick up the sticky, and partly bloody glass pieces. I drop the flute's broken glass back onto the hardwood floor, and stare at the bubbling alcohol.

I look back up at the small marble countertop that belonged to an even smaller kitchen island. I hate New York studio apartments. Lazily, with my sticky, wet, and bloody hands, I grab the champagne bottle. I take a sip… a rather large drink out of the bottle, and set it back on the countertop. I attempted to pick up the pieces again, but instead place my cut and uncut hands on my lap.

Blood soaking into my black jeans. But it's okay, it's not like anyone would be able to see.

I sigh and I could feel the coolness and smell of the sweet French liquid leave my breath.

I look up at the marble countertop again, my eyes glossy, and swiftly grab the bottle. Or so I thought I did swiftly. The blue, French, bottle falls and breaks on the clear champagne flute. I look at my cut hand and see the small shard of glass stuck in my finger.

''Dammit'' I whisper to myself and can still feel the cold champagne leave my lips. I take the piece of glass out, and toss it into the pool of champagne.

Tired and depressed I lay in the champagne. My blood, and hair mixing in with the champagne covered floors.

Pieces of my hair sticking to my forehead. Only a few tears escaping.

May 19th, 2023
[Edit times: 9:06 — 9:28 P.M.]
January 20th, 2024
[For the rewrites]
8:45 — 9:30
[For all of the edits]
Author's note:
It's the same thing with 'Beautiful'

However I didn't expect to foreshadow my life. Except for the interrupted ending. That part is not true. And this didn't take place in New York, it's Seattle and Tacoma, actually Renton and Tacoma. This story was originally called Champagne Problems. Hence all the champagne problems references. This was before I found out the real reason why M.F. cancelled on our first date.

Quotes

Right Person, Wrong Time — M.F.
'' I am a 'right person, wrong time' kind
Of girl. I met my right person, and it was
The wrong time. His past was coming back to
Haunt him, and my future, my life was coming back
To save me. But he still left me when I needed him
the most.''

Unrequited Love — G.L.H
'' I had an unrequited love before.
He wasn't mine to keep. And he
Wasn't mine to lose. But I repaired
His heart so he could love the next girl.
And he broke mine so I could hate the next boy.''

Last Poem

Beautiful July

From the day I became
Alive. To the day my
Heart's bright, red light
Died. I can always fall,
Rely on beautiful July.

To the day I say goodbye.
I have the heat of July. The
Sun in my brown–red hair.
Have my bare skin be kissed
By the golden sun. Never say
Goodbye to the fun I'm having
With them.

I'll stand up in the red convertible,
Hanging onto the windshield. My long
Hair swaying in the warm wind. In
The golden daylight.

No, no, I don't think I'll ever
Be able to do it.

From the day I became alive,

To the day my heart's red light
Died. Don't matter what the
Crime is. I'll never say goodbye.
To beautiful July.

Because why?

So I sunbathe in the golden
Sun. Have meaningful fun, with
Them. To the day I say goodbye.
I have beautiful July.

The sun in my brown–red
Hair. Have my bare skin
Be kissed by the golden sun.
And I'll never say goodbye
To the fun with them.

Oh how I love beautiful July.
Running, and doing everything,
In the heat of beautiful July.

December 11th, 2023, Monday
1:35 A.M. — 1:49 A.M.

Fallen In Love

[Sneak peak]

[Chapter One]

Chapter One

Pike Place Love.

Seattle was a beautiful city. On the outside.

It was beautiful inside too. If you just took all the cars, people, and litter away. I was in downtown Seattle on this beautiful sunny day. I didn't feel as beautiful as the outside looked.

 I had to go to my mother's work in downtown Seattle. I try to look at the best parts of this day though. I got to ride the light rail. I always liked to put in my earbuds, play music, and look out the window whenever I rode the light rail. It made me feel like I was in a movie.

And when I got off the light rail a breeze slightly blew through my hair while I listened to music. It was the perfect movie-like feel. I've yet to do it in the rain, I feel like that would be better. I walk the few steps and round the corner of the street to my mom's office, walking just a few more steps. Opening the big glass doors. I go up the escalator, walking to the last office in the hallway. When the receptionist sees me, she smiles.

''Hi, Valerie, your mom should be out soon.''

I smile back at the receptionist before I say, ''Okay, thank you, Andy.'' I turn my head and I see my mom's cubicle. ''Oh, there she is.'' My mom tosses her head up at me, I give her a small smile back.

''Oh! She is.'' Andy says back.

''You got here a lot earlier than I expected.'' My mother says as she walks towards me.

''I caught an earlier train.'' The train ride from the station was a thirty-five minute ride from my house to downtown, Westlake, specifically. I wanted to know what it would feel like if I was early to one of my appointments at my mother's office. Instead of on-time or a minute late.

''Well we're not quite ready for you yet. Another patient is finishing up. You can sit in the break room for a half-hour if you want. Snack on something.'' Sometimes I wished my mother acted this nice in general. She'd say it's my fault and that I have an attitude. Which could be true sometimes. But also sometimes it wasn't me, and she didn't see it.

''Can I go to Pike Place Market?'' I asked, hoping that she'd say yes.

''I don't know, it's dangerous. I don't like the idea of you going there by yourself. It's not that I don't trust you, it's just people are crazy in Seattle.'' She wasn't wrong, but I didn't want to sit in the break room. I knew that as soon as my appointment was done I was going to sit in there and eat peach Greek yogurt. Which I didn't mind, but I wanted to *so* badly go to Pike Place.

''Please, I'm just right around the corner, and I'll leave as soon as something seems off.'' I was going to give up if she said no, and just go to the break room in defeat.

''Just let her go, she's old enough now, Casey.'' Andy said, as she took my side. I smile.

''Okay, fine. You can go.'' I cheer a quiet yes, and ask my mother for some money so I can buy flowers. She sucked her teeth and I smiled wider. ''I don't know if I have any cash with me. If I do, sure.''

''Yay, thank you.'' I say, she says you're welcome, and I go into her locker in the break room and get the few bills she had in her wallet. Two tens and a five. I took the five for a sweet treat I thought she and I could share from my favourite bakery.

Since it was Tuesday the market wasn't that busy and not many cool things would be there. But the flowers would be there. The flowers were always there. I walked through the market happy as a clam, my smile and happiness buzzed like a bumble bee. I don't know why I was always happy to be at the market but it was my favourite part of Seattle. Always has, always will.

I almost passed it, but when I saw it I did a double take. I saw the most beautiful bouquet of daffodils. They were the perfect golden shade, and the baby's breath flowers were scattered. The bouquet was wrapped in paper that had the 'old newspaper' look. I'm sure nonsense was written on it but I didn't care. Something told me I couldn't let those flowers go. I had to buy them.

''Would you like to buy those?'' An elderly man said. I looked up at him and smiled.

''Yes, please. How much?'' The man paused and looked down at the flowers.

''Tell you what, I'll give them to you for ten dollars.''

''Oh, really? Thank you so much!'' I hand the man the ten dollar bill. I thank him again, and wish him a good day. I got to Le Panier, my favourite bakery in Seattle and ordered two raspberry macarons.

When I was walking back to my mom's work I bumped into someone. I saved my flowers. *Hopefully.* ''I am so sorry.'' The guy said.

I apologise too. ''No, I'm sorry. I should be looking where I'm walking and not the sky and architecture.'' I laugh the last part out.

The boy who kind of resembled Jeremy Irvine and a mix of someone else, I just can't put my finger on it. It's on the tip of my tongue too. Says back. ''Me too. I should've looked, I was looking at the buildings too.'' Joe Keery! That's who he reminded me of! The boy was a mixture of Joe Keery and Jeremy Irvine.

''I didn't know I was hungry for someone to love me, til you were on a plate.'' the song by Julia Michaels played through one of my earbuds. ''I'm Grey.'' The boy extended his hand. I put mine in his, then we shook hands.

''I'm Valerie.'' The lyrics, the boy, and the scenery. It all felt too unreal to be real. ''Are you a tourist? Visiting Pike Place, or do you work here?'' I shouldn't've asked the last question. He was dressed in a black blazer, white button-up shirt, jeans and dress shoes. He obviously didn't work here.

''I just came by from work, you?''

''I'm just here while waiting for my appointment at my mother's work.''

''Oh, sweet.'' The boy paused, looking at me intently. I do the same. Frozen in what to say next. ''How old are you?''

''Eighteen.'' I don't know why I felt like that was a lie. I *was* eighteen, but saying it tasted bitter. It was weird to say it more than be it. ''You?''

''Twenty-one.'' I said a small oh, while I nodded my head up and down twice. ''Can I get your number, Valerie?'' The way he said my name, made me compelled to give him my number.

''Yeah, of course.'' I ripped some of the fake newspaper paper off my flower bouquet that was thankfully safe, and grabbed a pen from my bag writing my number that started with the very famous 206.

It had been a day since I met Grey and gave him my number. He hadn't texted me, and I didn't know if he was ever going to. It was fine with me though, it didn't hurt.

I was downstairs and was watching T.V., everyone was upstairs and getting ready for bed. That's when I got a ping on my phone.

Grey: Hey it's Grey

Grey: Probably don't remember me because it's been soooo long

I smile at my phone. He texted me!

Valerie: Don't worry, I remember you

Grey and I texted for a few minutes, until he said we should go on a date. I froze and butterflies banged against my stomach. I've been asked on dates before, but I've always rejected the guys who asked me on a date. I wasn't comfortable going on dates with them. But for some reason, Grey made me comfortable. I *wanted* to go on a date with him. I'd just hope he didn't murder me.

I agree to a date, and tell Grey that I was nervous because I'd never been on a date. He explains how a date works. I roll my eyes. He kind of annoys me, but I like him. I told Grey that I knew how dates work, that I'd just never been on one.

Grey asks if I'm busy, I say no. He FaceTimes me. We talked for maybe an hour before he decided he needed to go to bed. It just took one look before I knew I liked this boy. I wanted to be his friend, I wanted to go on this date. I wanted to do whatever he wanted, talk about whatever he wanted. I just wanted him in my life, and in a way he is.

I'm happy I went to Pike Place. I almost didn't, but I did. *I did.* That's all that matters. When the clock struck 12:57 A.M. I turned off the lamp that was next to the couch, and pet my cat's head. I turn off the T.V. and kiss my cat's head, wishing him a goodnight. I turn off the dining room light.

When I go into my room I turn on the light, doing my nightly routine with music playing in my earbuds. When I walked back into my room from the bathroom, I switched into my pyjamas which just meant a T-shirt and my track shorts. I turn off my bedroom light. My room was then illuminated in a warm, soft, white light from my butterfly lights.

When I started to decorate my walls I wanted to go for a cottage core and 'fairyland' look. I bought fake roses and leaves. I wrapped the roses around my bed frame and all around my wall. It didn't look the way I wanted. It wasn't nearly as pretty in reality as I pictured it in my head. But I made do with what I had.

I climb under the blankets that were on top of my bed. I look around my room. And across my bed was my window, my dresser in the corner, and plain walls, minus the one with roses above my bed. My books underneath the burgundy chair that I'd gotten from my Nana.

I roll my eyes, at the hatred of my room. Bad memories trailed and floated in this room like driftwood in a lake.

I look at my phone. The time read 1:30 A.M., August 2nd. I smile.

Goodbye, July. Hello August. And this time I meant it.

To be continued…

Every Part Of Me

[Sneak peak]

Chapter Two]

Chapter Two

Lover

One Year ago / Age 19 & 23

Coffee shops were where I spent most of my time, as a nineteen-year-old wannabe singer. I would sit on a stool in front of two microphones, one for me, and one for my guitar. And sometimes I would get a piano. Those were for *special occasions*. They meant the most to me, because every time I had that piano at my fingertips the world glowed brighter and the stars aligned. Just for *him* and I.

I clear my throat to get the attention of the coffee shop people, who all look at me with curious, rude, and even side-eyes. I clear my throat again, but this time anxiously. ''Hi, I'm Emery Golden. I would like to thank Lavender Love cafe for inviting me once again.'' I paused and looked at the owner and she smiled and nodded her head. ''I am your typical nineteen-year-old who wants to be something and leave my hometown. Like every other depressed young adult out there.'' A few people laugh. ''Okay sorry, I'm a singer not a comedian. So this first song was inspired by an ex, like most great songs are, this song is called You Never Loved Me.''

Some people in the crowd cheered. Some gave a look that said 'you'll never make it.' Or 'you're not good, I already know'. I try to ignore them. I strum the chords of my guitar and after the first chorus I felt my anxiety melt away. I was singing the last verse of my song when the Lavender Love cafe's door chimed, signalling someone walking in.

With my eyes shut I sing out:

''*I guess out of sight don't always mean out of mind*

Cause the everythings that made you and I are all around me.''

Then I saw him, smiling at me, with this soft look. His eyes, his smile, his… good looking face… They were all so… soft. I couldn't help but give him that same soft look.

''*Lover*'' —oops. ''*You're all around me*

Like Saturn's rings. And you're not even around me.'' I finished. The man looks at me and claps loudly, maybe even the loudest, with the crowd.

I thank the crowd and tell them I'll be back after a short intermission. And I walk to the counter.

''Good job Emery.'' The barista behind the counter tells me.

''Thanks, Emily. Can I have my usual please? A peach arnold palmer.'' In short that's what it was. It was just —sweetened—black tea, lemonade, and peach juice.

''Peach Arnie, with extra peach juice coming right up!''

''Thank you, how much this time?''

''I got it!'' The man with the *lover's* look tells Emily. I look at Emily, and back at *lover*.

''Oh… then what would you like sir?''

''I'll get the same thing,'' *lover* looks at me. With that same soft smile. The same soft… everything. ''I trust your taste.''

''And that my good sir, would be your first miss-taste—'' I chuckled as I heard how it didn't sound funny at all. ''Sorry, that sounded better in my head.''

''Yeah you should buy me a drink instead, for my poor ears.''

''Next time, I'm going to enjoy my free peach Arnie today.''

''I'm Jack Mariam Fischer.'' He holds out his hand. As he states his full name.

''Emery Venice Golden.'' I say mine, mocking him, and I take his hand. His touch felt… right. Like he was just for me.

After ten more minutes of talking to Jack, and setting up for the last two songs of my set. Where I introduce myself again for the new people of the cafe, and thank the owner of Lavender Love, again. To which she smiles.

When I finished and was cleaning up, the cafe had about another hour of it being open. So I decided that I would get another peach Arnie. I had just closed my guitar in its case, when *Jack Fischer* cleared his throat to get my attention. When I faced him he still had that soft look on his face.

"Do you perform here a lot?" He asks.

"Uh, yeah I guess I would, yeah." Words and sentences became unknown when he got into my peripheral.

"It was nice to meet you again, Emery." Jack holds his hand for me to take, again.

"You too, Jack." I match his smile.

When Jack slipped his hand away from mine I felt a glimpse of emptiness, and I didn't like it. But the crinkle of paper in our untwined hands made my heart skip a beat. When his red flannel cladded back faces me I open the slightly crinkled paper.

Sing me a song and I'll fall in love

When I looked up from the piece of paper to look for Jack, he was gone.

To be continued…

Acknowledgments

All thanks to the Taylor Swift songs/other songs
that inspired some of the poems/songs.
And I guess to my best friend Leah.
(she'll get it).
Here is the songs that inspired/ I listened to when I
wrote these

Dress –Taylor Swift — Dress

Best –Gracie Abrams — I'm Sorry That I Miss You

Haunted, Clean, All You Had To Do Was Stay
–Taylor Swift — Until You Had Me

Cornelia Street, Death By A Thousand Cuts, Call It
What You Want –Taylor Swift — Alki Beach

Is It Over Now?, Now That We Don't Talk –Taylor
Swift — Fool's Gold

Lacy –Noah Kahan (Cover) — Every Part Of Me
(Elegant)

Getaway Car –Taylor Swift — Getaway Car (No, I
didn't mean to title it that. I was listening to
Getaway Car, and remembered how M.F. promised
we could go on a trip, in his banged up gold car, aka
the 'getaway car'. Hence all the credit I've been
giving Taylor)

Halloween –Noah Kahan — Noah Kahan

You're Losing Me –Taylor Swift — Gorgeous

Safe & Sound –Taylor Swift — I Didn't Deserve This

History Of Man –Maisie Peters — The Louvre (French)

''Slut!'' –Taylor Swift — You Were My Home

Ivy –Taylor Swift — Incandescent Glow

www.ingramcontent.com/pod-product-compliance
Lightning Source LLC
Chambersburg PA
CBHW061435160726
47995CB00003B/898